VOLUME 3

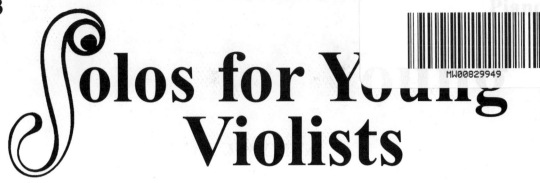

Solos for Young Violists

Compiled and Edited by Violist **Barbara Barber**

Viola by Christian Pederson, Albuquerque, 2002
From the collection of Robertson & Sons Violin Shop Inc., Albuquerque, NM
Photo by Justin Robertson

© 1997 Summy-Birchard Music
a division of Summy-Birchard, Inc.
Exclusive print rights administered by Alfred Publishing Co., Inc.
All Rights Reserved   Printed in USA

ISBN 1-58951-186-7

INTRODUCTION

Solos for Young Violists is a five-volume series of music books with companion CDs featuring 34 works for viola and piano. Many of the pieces in this collection have long been recognized as stepping stones to the major viola repertoire, while others are newly discovered, arranged and published for this series; most are premier recordings. Compiled, edited and recorded by violist Barbara Barber, *Solos for Young Violists* is a graded series of works ranging from elementary to advanced levels and represents an exciting variety of styles and techniques for violists. The collection has become a valuable resource for teachers and students of all ages. The piano track recorded on the second half of each CD gives the violist the opportunity to practice with accompaniments.

Contents

Alleluja

from Exsultate, jubilate, K. 165

W. A. Mozart
1756-1791
Arranged by Barbara Barber

* The smaller notes may be omitted.

Fantasia on Greensleeves

Adapted from the opera *Sir John in Love*

R. Vaughan Williams
1872-1958
Arranged by Watson Forbes

D
33 Allegretto (𝅗𝅥 = 𝅗𝅥.) ♩=126 "Lovely Joan"
p espressivo
8va
fpp
una corda
6
Ped.
sempre lontano
35
(8va)
37
(8va)
3
loco
39

14

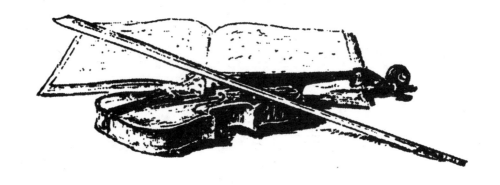

*"Let the love for literature,
painting, sculpture, architecture,
and, above all, music
enter into your lives."*

—Theodore Roosevelt

Romanian Peasant Dance, Op. 15

Dans Țărănesc

Constantin Dimitrescu
1847-1928
Arranged by R. Vidas & B. Barber

poco rit.

B

a tempo

(To Coda 2nd time)

pizz.

Gavotte
Op. 132, No. 1

Hans Sitt
1850-1922

D.C. al Fine

Mazurka
Op. 132, No. 2

Hans Sitt
1850-1922

D.C. al Fine

Divertimento
3rd Movement

Franz Joseph Haydn
1732-1809
Transcribed by Gregor Piatigorsky

Sonatina
for Viola and Piano

I

William Keith Rogers
1921-

Andante con moto ♩. = 58

II

III

Allegro commodo ♩ = 108